VILLAS
AND PALACES OF
EUROPE

Adalberto Dal Lago

VILLAS
AND PALACES OF
EUROPE

CASSELL
LONDON

Cassell Publishers Limited
Artillery House, Artillery Row
London SW1P 1RT

Translated from the Italian original
Ville antiche

© Gruppo Editoriale Fabbri, Bompiani, Sonzogno, Etas S.p.A., Milan 1966,
1984

This edition 1988

British Library Cataloguing in Publication Data
Dal Lago, Adalberto
Villas and palaces of Europe. — (Cassell's styles in art).
1. Europe. Large residences. Architectural features, ca 1400-ca 1850
I. Title   II. Ville antiche. *English*
728.8'094

ISBN 0-304-32178-8

Printed in Italy by Gruppo Editoriale Fabbri S.p.A., Milan

CONTENTS

Page

INTRODUCTION

The subject of this study calls for an introductory passage to define its terms of reference and describe the methods which have been used.

It must be pointed out that the heritage of secular architecture in Europe is so rich that any attempt to catalogue it would be futile. For this reason I have decided to present a number of examples, illustrating the development of the villa in all its aspects—including technology, individual characteristics and formal lay-out—from the beginning of the Renaissance to the 18th century.

Italian examples predominate among the buildings described because this type of architecture reached such heights in Italy that it has to be treated as a typically Italian development, especially during the period covered by the present study.

In considering the architecture of the villa in Europe, it is important to remember its evolution from the earlier fortress in France, England and

Germany. This had an important effect on the appearance of villas in these countries, and was the reason for their different characteristics. In the whole period under consideration, the aim has been as far as possible to study buildings situated outside the urban environment. The 'villa' has been envisaged as a special type of house in which deliberate emphasis on the relationship between architecture and natural surroundings brings about a kind of interaction of the two elements.

Actually—in Renaissance villas, for example—the town villa, too, frequently has this characteristically close relationship with its surroundings. But at the same time it has certain specifically urban features; these are important factors, sometimes heterogeneous, sometimes strongly marked by local influences.

Originally these buildings, which are now completely integrated into the urban fabric, were outside the boundaries of the city, which grew and finally absorbed them. The outskirts of Florence at the end of the 15th century were studded with estates and luxurious homes within a three-mile radius. Similarly, 18th-century London was surrounded by a ring of small summer residences.

The study of the villa involves two different problems: the definition of the term 'villa', and the relationship between this type of building and its natural surroundings. More specifically, this involves study of the transformations of the relationship between artificial and natural surroundings brought about by man's changing attitudes to nature.

The Classical world's view of nature was mythological and allegorical; the very plants and gardens were shaped in geometrical patterns, arranged to reproduce a natural effect. Man's natural surroundings were envisaged as an ideal setting in which he might find the best possible conditions for life on earth.

In the Middle Ages nature was regarded as essentially enclosed, inaccessible and unspoilt. Later, the viewpoint changed: nature was no longer a symbol of supernatural reality, but rather the reflection of man's own nature, worthy of study and interest, and with a special bearing on man's handiwork.

During the Renaissance, a conception of nature as regular and ordered co-existed with the feeling that it was full of surprises and new creations, and closely related to man's mood.

The Romantics saw nature not as influenced by man, but rather as itself influencing man, leading him back to beauty and goodness. This belief is incarnate in the English garden, which tended to eliminate the

distinction between cultivated and uncultivated landscapes, remoulding nature only in order to reveal
its beauty.

HISTORY OF THE VILLA

To call one particular type of dwelling a villa raises
the problem of architectural terminology, for to
mention examples entails identifying 'types' of villa.
This is really only a meaningful activity when
undertaken in connection with study of specific
historical traditions or contents, whether cultural,
social, religious, economic, or technological. It is
therefore necessary to recapitulate briefly the development of the villa.

The first real villa of the ancient world was the
Roman villa of Republican and Imperial times. 'This
is hard to classify into types', writes Luciano Pontuale
in the *Enciclopedia dell' Arte* (vol. XIII, 1965) 'because
of the freedom with which the numerous and varied
architectural units are combined.' The villa evolved
from a rural type, still restricted to a more or less compact block (Catullus's villa at Sirmione), to more
fluid ground-plans (the villas of Pompeii and
Herculaneum). The Roman villa embraced the

whole farm—the land, the workers' quarters, the stables, the hay-lofts and all the farm buildings, as well as the place where the owner lived.

Even in Republican times, however, a gradual differentiation occurred between the rustic villa and the land-owner's villa, though this remained a simple building consisting of a few rooms and a bath. During the Imperial period the villa underwent important changes, and all the features of the old patrician rural *domus* disappeared. The building was divided into south and north wings, each of which had matching alcoves and rooms for rest and recreation. The grounds became more spacious, and servants' quarters were enlarged. Building on several floors was another feature.

During the Imperial period the character of the villa underwent further changes, and its different parts came to be freely connected according to the requirements of the site and landscape. The great villas of the late Empire were spacious; it was no longer necessary to plan buildings to a rigidly pre-determined formula. Alongside this type of 'suburban villa', which served mainly as a dwelling, there grew up the 'rural villa', designed for efficient administration of an estate, and including modest accommodation for the owner, whose visits would only be short. Such villas have architectural features which are very different from those of the suburban villa, and equally remote from the typical ground-plan of the Roman *domus*.

Towards the end of the Empire, after the first Barbarian invasions, villas fell into disuse. It was many centuries before they reappeared. The castle replaced the villa, and in the 13th and 14th centuries its structure and design were in turn the starting-point from which the suburban villa of the modern period evolved.

For this reason it is worth briefly summarising the general design of the castle. Its component parts were the surrounding wall, the keep or stronghold, and the living-quarters. It was enclosed by a strong, usually rectangular, wall with towers at the corners and surrounded by a moat. The residential quarters were originally extremely simple and limited. Later, a special approach (drawbridge) was added, as well as an inner courtyard which linked the rooms in an almost unchanging pattern.

Not until the early Renaissance did a type of fortified house appear in Italy. Many foreign influences helped to determine its form, including the French and Germans in northern Italy and the Saracens, Normans and Hohenstaufen emperors in the south.

The Italian castle was quickly transformed into a mansion which was no longer built for defence but for enjoyment. The suburban villa reappeared.

During the 13th century dwellings of this kind were still very rare (the villa Rufolo at Ravello, near Naples, is an example); but in the 14th century, particularly in the neighbourhood of Florence, it was again common for the richer citizens to own villas. In the Middle Ages the house with a garden did not differ in any essential respect (except its rarity) from other homes; but in this century, and above all in Italy, it again became a distinctive architectural entity.

The villas of northern and central Italy often preserve recognisable structural and stylistic features of the old farm-houses (Careggi, Cafaggiolo). Roman villas, on the other hand, broke completely with the past; their gardens are integrated physically as well as aesthetically with the main building by means of porches and stairways. (Examples are Vignola's Villa Farnese at Caprarola and Pirro Ligorio's Villa d'Este at Tivoli.) In Tuscany these new buildings, while retaining the tower, courtyard, loggia and small walled garden, are simple constructions designed for plain living over many months of each year.

Many of these villas show traces of their derivation from the fortified house. Almost all have the central courtyard; loggias and main rooms are often frescoed; the façades are plainly designed and almost invariably distempered with a chalk wash; and stone is used around the doors, windows and corners. The villas of Latium, and particularly those of Rome, belong to a later date, and their features are different from those of Tuscan villas. Roman villas are always built in a commanding position, with wide views over the countryside, and stately stairways, porticos, and imposing proportions. Their façades are full of contrast, with deep colonnades, recesses and porches. Roman villas are so numerous and varied that it is hard to generalise about their ground-plans, which are extremely complex; some were designed on the lines of Classical *thermae* (public baths).

Villas in and around Genoa, the finest examples of which were built during the early Renaissance, consist of a compact, square building on three floors: ground floor, *piano nobile,* and above this the *sottotetto.* There is still a tower, sometimes part of the main building, sometimes detached. Loggias are used to lighten the façades. The entrance-hall on the ground floor leads to several side rooms; the first floor has the main reception room and smaller rooms.

During the 15th and 16th centuries the influence of French architecture in Piedmont caused the fortified house to be transformed into a residential house; but it retained all the characteristics of the castle.

In this period, country houses were of minor architectural importance. They were rustic productions, descended from farmhouses.

In Lombardy the villa evolved as it did in Piedmont. Situated along the shores of the lakes, in Brianza or the Bergamo district, the villas of Lombardy are more interesting for the complexity of their ground-plans than for the design of their façades or their decorative detail.

From the early Renaissance period, the custom of living in the country transformed numerous castles in the Veneto into dwelling-houses, though these retained their Medieval features. The exceptional affluence of Venetian society allowed the development of a type of villa which the work of artists like Palladio, Scamozzi and Sanmicheli gave great architectural importance. A detailed description of Venetian villas will be given later, but at this point it is worth mentioning certain features, for these buildings became famous throughout Europe, and influenced villa architecture right down to the 20th century.

Working in the Veneto, Palladio was the first European architect to achieve an intimate relationship between a building and its landscape, conceived as integrated and reciprocally dependent elements. For the first time, the main axes of a building are extended without a break into the surrounding landscape.

Almost all Palladio's buildings were country houses — reflecting the fact that, from the Renaissance onwards, secular architecture was just as much a matter of artistic concern as religious architecture. Palladio's country houses did not offer the comfort of those of northern Europe or of English manor houses, but they still achieved impressive, though unostentatious, effects.

The Palladian style, still used in Italy in the 18th century (for example the Villa Albani, Rome), spread throughout Europe. It spread to France, where its practitioners included the architects Gabriel, Ledoux, Chalgrin and Soufflot; to Russia in the person of the architect Quarenghi; and to England, where Palladio's Rotonda is copied almost exactly at Mereworth (near Tonbridge), at Chiswick House, and at Nuthall Temple, Nottinghamshire. The Palladian style subsequently reached the North American colonies.

In this way the villa-palazzo — traditional and

sober in mood during the Renaissance, impressive and monumental in the Baroque period—spread throughout Europe, though more rustic country houses continued to exist alongside it. Italian architecture was the dominant influence on the evolution of the villa, which was not fully developed in the rest of Europe until the late 17th and 18th centuries. Numerous Italian architects, particularly those from Lombardy and the Grisons, worked at the Austrian, German and Russian courts.

In France the country mansion remained a modified form of the Medieval castle. The *maisons de plaisance* were derived from this original too, with external and internal proportions duly reduced. During the 18th century, however, a special type of country house developed, with a ground-plan derived partly from the Medieval castle and partly from the *hôtel* of town life.

In England and Holland too, the country house was for several centuries a kind of fortified house. The influence of Palladian architecture and the French *hôtels* on English architecture was widely felt, as can be seen from 16th-century buildings, which are compact and symmetrical, with carefully calculated proportions. The interiors, too, are accurately defined, in accordance with the English tradition, which was to influence the design of domestic architecture not only in Europe but above all in America.

In Germany there are few examples of 16th-century villas. Towards the second half of the 17th century, vastly-proportioned, highly complicated mansions were built, the design being entrusted to Italian artists—Viscardi and Gabrieli in Bavaria, Chiaveri at Dresden, Retti at Stuttgart.

French influence was strongly felt in the Rhineland. The castles of Nymphenburg, Benrath and Monrepos are huge; they illustrate all the grandiose and magnificent characteristics of Baroque architecture.

Under Peter the Great (1682–1725), large mansions in a notably Palladian style were built in Russia. This occurred through the influence of the many Italian architects, including Rastrelli, Camporesi, Gilardi and Quarenghi, who worked there. Nor was all the work done at Moscow and St Petersburg: Quarenghi worked at Tula and Kiev, Gilardi at Kharkov.

In the 19th century a multitude of styles existed side by side in Europe. Nikolaus Pevsner has called the period 'the fancy-dress ball' of architecture. Villa architecture adopted the most varied styles—Neo-Gothic, Neo-Classical, 'Indian', 'Moorish'—in a hotch-potch of different forms and shapes which had no relevance to their particular architectural context or their surroundings.

After the First World War, a new architectural style appeared, created by a small number of highly imaginative and creative architects. There had not been such an important architectural revolution since the time, five hundred years before, when the pioneers of the Renaissance had abandoned the Gothic style to create a new visual language.

Thus the Modern Movement in architecture was born. Steel, glass and reinforced concrete were the new materials. The ground-plan and appearance of the villa—like that of other buildings—underwent a violent transformation corresponding to a new conception of the relationship between architecture and nature.

The problem of the relationship between the villa and its surroundings has already been mentioned. The relationship between villa and garden design involves discussion of both the aesthetics of garden design and the changes in man's attitude towards nature.

The Renaissance was one such change in the relationship between man and nature; consequently the natural element—the park or garden—became the integrating feature of villa design. A study of the architecture of this period precludes a clear-cut distinction between the building and its surroundings; from now on the two are closely related.

During the 14th and 15th centuries the main characteristic of gardens was naturalism—that is, the natural element was arranged in complete formal freedom. Unchanged by man, it takes its place within an exact formal plan.

At the end of the 15th century, and even more so in the 16th century, certain rational, anti-natural features were introduced into garden design; these modified the form of the garden, and shaped its outline in accordance with an accurate geometrical plan. Starting from the postulate that rationality and beauty coincide, the Renaissance developed its own instruments of control, using theories of symmetry and mathematical proportion like the theories of the golden mean, and of the relationship between human proportions and universal harmony.

The villa developed from the fortified into the residential dwelling, and many great architects became landscape-gardeners: Michelozzo built the Villa Medici at Careggi and Il Trebbio at Cafaggiolo; Sangallo built the Villa Medici at Poggio a Caiano; and so on. The garden became one of the most common architectural features. Raphael, Bramante, Peruzzi and Vignola devoted themselves to designing open spaces with a wide variety of purposes. There were new principles of subdividing space, of treating space polycentrically instead of centrally (reflecting, perhaps, the discoveries of Copernicus and the teachings of Galileo).

The garden became a wonderful and fantastic place; trees became more important once their contribution to the beauty of the scene was recognised. The gardens of the Villa Ludovisi, of the Villa Doria Pamphili, and the Villa Corsini are the most famous in central Italy. From there the Italian style of garden design spread throughout Europe; its fundamental characteristics were repeated at Fontainebleau, at Hampton Court, and later in Spain, Austria and Russia.

Not until the 18th century did a new style arise— from the experiments of Le Notre in the planning of buildings and arrangement of surrounding spaces. And even this had its roots in the Italian Baroque tradition. He altered their interrelationships and created a new style which spread throughout Europe and America. The gardens of Vaux-le-Vicomte and Versailles are wonderful examples of his work.

The garden front of the palace of Versailles faces

the magnificent park with its vast flower-beds, its views of water at right-angles, its fountains, glades which seem to stretch on for ever in parallel or radiating lines, and its paths between tall hedges. Nature herself is adapted by man to further the glory of the king, whose bedroom lies at the centre of the whole complex.

The garden of the castle of Schönbrunn, planned by Fischer von Erlach in 1694, was arranged according to principles derived from Le Notre's work; but though all the features used by the great French architect (stairways, *parterres,* terraces) are present, the prevailing impression is that of a limitless park.

A different attitude to nature prevailed in England, and led to important changes in garden planning. A new style, 'the English garden', expressing pictorial and scenic interests, was introduced.

The fundamental cultural revolution brought about by the Modern Movement entailed the transformation not only of the villa but also of its surroundings. Dimensional unity between architecture and landscape, and spatial continuity between interior and exterior were the new features introduced.

The present volume deals with one period of architectural change, and an extremely significant one: the evolution of the villa from the Renaissance to the beginning of the Modern Movement.

THE ITALIAN RENAISSANCE

The revolution in art and thought which we call the Renaissance began in the 15th century in Florence. The first phase began in about 1420 and lasted until the end of the 15th century; two further periods spanned the entire 16th century.

The Renaissance was marked by swift developments in secular architecture. Whereas the predominantly religious architecture of the Middle Ages had usually been carried out by groups of master-builders and only exceptionally by individual artists, Renaissance buildings were strongly individual enterprises in which the architect expressed his own personality.

In the 15th and 16th centuries vast private fortunes were invested in building the palaces and villas which took the place of the Medieval castles. Town life offered greater efficiency and security, but the country villa regained its old character as a peaceful and beautiful setting for the cultivated man, with the garden as an integral part of the scene.

The confidence, affluence and aesthetic awareness introduced by the Medici led to the building of the first Renaissance villas in Florence. Their model was Cosimo de' Medici's villa at Careggi.

In 15th- and 16th-century Lombardy residential dwellings evolved from castles. The character of such buildings was substantially changed by influences which came chiefly from central Italy, and certain functional features were reintroduced. In this district, however, famous architects were not to be found working specifically on country houses. (Contrast the work of Alessi in Liguria, and of Vignola, Sangallo, Raphael and Peruzzi in central Italy.)

Renaissance villas in Lombardy include the Villa Castelbarco at Robecco, the Villa Litta at Trenzanesio, the Villa Gallarati-Scotti at Arcore, the Villa Cicogna at Bisuschio, and the Mirabello and the Bicocca at Milan.

The Mirabello and the Bicocca, surviving examples of 15th-century Milanese villas, are mainly interesting because of their influence on architectural ideas, which was strong because they were situated inside the urban network. The Villa Mirabello (plates 1 and 2) was designed for recreation, hunting and farming. It is built to an L-shaped ground-plan, with brick-covered façades which are broken by numerous arched terracotta windows. On the ground-floor, facing the garden, are three stone-columned arcades. On the second floor, there is a large loggia—a feature clearly borrowed from local tradition, which strongly influenced both the appearance and the ground-plans of all buildings of the period. The Arcimboldi's Bicocca (plate 3) belongs to the late 15th-century type of country house. On the ground-floor there is a portico with five arches; a large belvedere on the top floor is lit by an open gallery on all four sides.

The Villa Cicogna at Bisuschio (plates 9 and 10) represents an advance on preceding villas, and was built in the 15th century as a hunting-lodge for the Mozzoni family. A hundred years later it was re-modelled and decorated by the Campi brothers, painters of the School of Cremona. It is an outstanding example of the Renaissance villa in Lombardy, and bears witness to the influence of Tuscan and Roman architecture on the Lombard style.

The loggias of the wings, which reach out into the garden, resemble features which are commonly found in Tuscany; and the vaulted ceilings are frescoed with pergolas and vines like those of Pope Julius's villa in Rome. The building is surrounded by a splendid garden, and the different levels of the hillside are used to advantage, so that each floor of the house leads out to a different part of the garden. Other notable features are the arcaded underground galleries and a staircase, one of the finest in Italy, which leads into the garden. The arrangement of the villa around a courtyard which is open on one side (facing garden, street and piazza) is characteristic of most Lombard villas which were originally castles. (In villas adapted from castles, one side of the original rectangular structure either disappeared or was pierced at ground-floor level by large arches.)

At Poggio a Caiano, between Florence and Pistoia, stands the Villa Medici (plate 14), which Lorenzo the Magnificent commissioned from Giuliano da Sangallo in 1479. It is situated on a hill giving a splendid view of the magnificent landscape around it. The villa was built by using and converting material from the Villa Ambra, which had belonged to the Strozzi and Rucellai families.

The work lasted five years. Giuliano da Sangallo surrounded the house with an arcade which forms a continuous balcony at first-floor level and provides a natural link between the building and the surrounding landscape. The nucleus of the villa is a large central barrel-vaulted hall, reaching to the roof, built on a system inspired by *thermae*. The building also shows signs of its derivation from the architecture of Imperial Rome in the way it is related to its surroundings. The porch, on the other hand, in spite of its extremely Classical appearance, includes features characteristic of the local tradition, influenced by Brunelleschi. The main block of the building is of a strong and simple geometrical form, and subtle perspective foreshortenings are used to project it into its surroundings by means of the arcade and the terrace above it.

The central hall, built where the inner courtyard is usually found, is the pivot of the whole building. It was completed by Leo X, who commissioned Andrea del Sarto and Franciabigio to decorate the main walls with frescos of episodes from the history of the Medici family. The entrance, which was a simple door in Lorenzo's time, was transformed into a stately portal. The frieze above the central loggia is the work of Della Robbia. Filippo Lippi and Alessandro Allori worked on the interior decoration later (1559). The garden was altered during the 19th century into a garden in the English style.

Other Tuscan villas built between the second half of the 15th century and the end of the 16th century are the Villa Medici at Cafaggiolo, the Villa of Artimino and La Petraia at Florence.

At Cafaggiolo (in the valley of the Mugello, a few miles from Florence), Cosimo il Vecchio commissioned Michelozzo di Bartolommeo to build a villa, later known as 'Il Trebbio' (plate 11). Il Trebbio was originally conceived as a hunting lodge. Built on a hill, with a magnificent view, it represents an attempt to combine Gothic features with those of the Renaissance. Michelozzo achieved this in other works as well, for example the Sacristy of Sta Trinita at Florence, the Church of the Bosco at i Frati, and the Villa Medici at Careggi.

At Cafaggiolo, and later at Careggi, the humanist ideal of the country house as a place of rest and spiritual refreshment was fulfilled. Lorenzo the Magnificent, Alberti, Brunelleschi, Donatello, and later Michelangelo stayed in this house, which testifies to the economic sway and artistic flair of the Medici.

The Villa of Artimino at Signa (plates 4 and 5) is built on a hill, in a vast pinewood. Ferdinand I commissioned it in 1594 from Buontalenti, whose plans blended the essential features of the fortified and the residential villa. He made both his ground-plan and the elevation of the villa fluid and dynamic, breaking up the façades with numerous windows. The villa is a refined creation—restrained, almost austere in appearance—and embodies the formal characteristics of the late Renaissance.

La Petraia (plates 6 and 7) stands on the site of a castle, from which the villa was built. It was executed for Francesco dei Medici by Buontalenti in 1575. The architect retained only the great tower from the existing building; it overlooks the whole Florentine plain.

The outside of the villa has a typically 16th-century harmony of design. The building is constructed around an inner courtyard—with distempered sides and a stone skirting-board at their base—whose walls are entirely covered with frescoes by Volterrano.

From the courtyard, which has a chapel nearby, one passes to the various reception rooms, which are arranged on a 16th-century plan. The garden (today arranged quite differently) was laid out in a manner typical of the period, and particularly of Florence. There are a number of fountains; the best known is at the foot of the rampart supporting the terrace in front of the villa. All the natural features are arranged in a picturesque design which is a triumph of the application of the rules of architecture to nature.

In 1547 Giacomo Barozzi, known as Vignola, built the Villa Farnese at Caprarola (plates 12 and 13) in a splendid position on the Cimini hills. He used the foundations constructed by Peruzzi and Sangallo for a castle in 1521, and the new work was done for Cardinal Alessandro Farnese, grandson of Paul III.

In this building the complete fusion of villa- and castle-architecture was achieved. The façades, the arrangement of the interior, and the round courtyard are certainly the work of Vignola. His youthful training, his experience of art in Rome and his stay in France were decisive influences on his artistic development, visible in this villa, which is his masterpiece. Although it has certain Mannerist features drawn from Bramante and Raphael, the Villa Farnese was a landmark in the growth of the Baroque style, and has an important place in the history of European architecture.

The exterior of the building illustrates Vignola's severity of style. The austere divisions of floors and surfaces and the impressive monumentality of the building are lightened by external flights of steps. The two stairways lead from the vast front courtyard to the imposing façade of the villa, which suggests its fortified origin. The centre of the main building is occupied by a semicircular court, surrounded by porticoes leading to the rooms on the ground and first floors. After a succession of salons decorated with

1. Villa Mirabello. 15th century. Milan.

2. The courtyard of the Villa Mirabello. 15th century. Milan.

3. Villa 'La Bicocca' 15th century. Milan.

4. Bernardo Buontalenti (1536-1608). Villa di Artimino.
Signa, Florence.

5. Bernardo Buontalenti (1536-1608). Villa di Artimino.
Signa, Florence.

6. Bernardo Buontalenti (1536-1608). Villa 'La Petraia'. Florence.

7. Bernardo Buontalenti (1536-1608). Villa 'La Petraia'. Florence.

8. Villa Gamberaia. Settignano, Florence.

9. Villa Cicogna. 15th century. Bisuschio, Milan.

10. Villa Cicogna. 15th century. Bisuschio, Milan.

11. Michelozzo Michelozzi (1396-1472). 'Il Trebbio'.
Cafaggiolo, Florence.

12. Giacomo Barozzi da Vignola (1507-1573). Villa Farnese. Caprarola, Viterbo.

13. Giacomo Barozzi da Vignola (1507-1573). Villa Farnese. Caprarola, Viterbo.

14. Giuliano da Sangallo (1445-1516). Villa Medici. Poggio a Caiano, Florence.

15. Baldassare Peruzzi (1481-1526). 'La Farnesina'. Rome.

16. Bartolomeo Ammanati (1511-1592), Giorgio Vasari (1511-1574), Giacomo Barozzi da Vignola (1507-1573). Villa Giulia. Rome.

frescoes by Vignola and Tempesta come the smaller rooms at the rear of the building, with doors opening on to bridges over the moat.

At the entrance there is a fountain; from this a steep grassy slope enclosed between walls descends to another fountain in a small amphitheatre leading to the casino and its garden—a real masterpiece, recalling the atmosphere of the Petit Trianon at Versailles.

In 1508 the banker Agostino Chigi commissioned Baldassare Peruzzi to work on the villa which came to be known as La Farnesina (plate 15) because it was later bought by Cardinal Alessandro Farnese, grandson of Paul III. The decoration of the interior was executed by Raphael, Giulio Romano, Giovanni da Udine and Sebastiano del Piombo.

The house is a 16th-century version of the suburban villa. It includes stylistic features dating from the years before Bramante and Raphael (such, for example, as were to be found in 15th-century Tuscan and Roman architecture), and is clearly the work of a refined and sensitive artist. It consists of a cube-shaped central block, dating from the 15th century, and two projecting wings at either side.

At almost the same time, Cardinal Giulio Medici, who was to become Pope Clement VII, was building the Villa Madama (plate 17) which, like the Farnesina, was intended for state receptions rather than private life. The work was planned by Raphael and completed by Sangallo. The original plan envisaged a series of loggias arranged round a circular courtyard. This would have provided the entrance to a theatre in the Greek style, hollowed out of the side of the hill on which the villa stood. The theatre and loggias would have helped to integrate the building with its surroundings; but the house was not completed on these lines. Today its façade is bare and plain. But the area inside the loggia is magnificently successful.

This explanation is essential to an understanding of the villa's visual meaning, which is connected with Raphael's other activities, both theoretical (studies of ancient monuments) and practical (his *Loggia* in the Vatican), and is reminiscent of the treatment of space in Roman Baths.

The construction of the villa was such as to ensure stability against possible movements of the hill caused by the amphitheatre and the terraces and gardens on different levels envisaged in the original plan.

Even the colonnade was not realised in accordance with the earliest plan. Nevertheless, the Villa Madama was an important achievement, and influenced Palladio's work in Venice; it was deeply expressive of the spirit of Renaissance man and his deep veneration for the Classical past.

Four architects collaborated on the plans for the Villa Giulia: Vasari, Ammanati, Vignola and Michelangelo, who supervised the work for Pope Julius III. The villa (plates 16) is on the Via Flaminia, in a narrow valley which drops down to the Tiber. Vasari is considered to have been responsible for the general design and Ammanati for the main building and the porticoed wing dividing the garden and courtyard from the *nympheum,* which Vignola planned.

The most notable architectural feature is the garden courtyard. Facing this is a semicircular frontage, with colonnades leading to the portico.

THE VENETIAN VILLA

A study of villa architecture must pay special attention to the design of Venetian villas, particularly in the 16th and 17th centuries. Between the middle of the 15th and the beginning of the 19th century, villa-building developed astonishingly in that part of the Italian mainland known as 'the three Venetias'. This resulted from a faith in traditional values and a common attitude which isolated the rural architecture of Venetia from changes in taste.

The special character of Venetian villas is largely derived from their agricultural function, which influenced both their ground-plans and the appearance of their exteriors. The typical Venetian villa consisted of a main building in which the owner lived, porticoed extensions at the sides called *barchesse* (farm buildings), a garden in the Italian style, a park in the background and a fishpond. These features are almost invariably present.

The interiors are comprised of a reception room, a dining-room, sometimes one or two smaller rooms, bedrooms and service rooms, which are often in the semi-basement. 'Their ground-plans', writes Liliana Balzaretti (*Ville Venete,* 1965), 'with their avoidance of complicated interconnections, demonstrate their descent from the traditional Venetian country house, as well as their search for building proportions that avoid the grandiose. The villa is given its peculiar character by the presence of the side porticoes (*barchesse*), which indicate its practical purpose and its rural origin, and immediately place it within the landscape. Their internal anatomy, their different heights and ground-levels achieve an intimate link with the surrounding landscape.'

The landscape is a fundamental feature of Venetian villa architecture. It is an essentially agricultural landscape, always taken into consideration by the designer of the ground-plan and elevations.

Different ground-levels, water-courses and trees were natural features which provided the setting within which the villa was placed; and the building's extremities, the *barchesse,* were extended in natural features (for example, hedges) which developed the design and assisted its integration with the landscape.

Palladio, Longhena, Sanmicheli and Scamozzi were the architects of the most famous of these villas. Between 1547 and 1549, Andrea Palladio built the Rotonda, the Villa Piovene at Lonido, the Villa Trissino at Meledo, and the Villa Pisani at Montagnana. Between about 1560 and 1570 he built the Villa Muzani at Caldogno, the Villa Poiana at Poiana Maggiore, the Villa Saraceno at Finale, the Villa Foscari at Mira, the Villa Emo Capodilista at Fonzolo, the Villa Sarego at Pedemonte, and the Villa Cornaro at Piombino Dese.

His output is astonishing—for as well as these buildings, the creations of his private architectural practice, he built public buildings in his capacity as overseer of the Basilica of Vicenza and later, on Sansovino's death, as overseer in Venice.

The early villas are of somewhat uncertain character; Palladio's mature works, built between 1560 and 1570, have complicated ground-plans, with façades centred on colonnaded porches, often with balconies above them. The porch is frequently squeezed into the façade because the volume of the building spreads to the side buildings and *barchesse* and thence to the surrounding landscape.

This integration of the building with its natural surroundings is always found in Palladio's work. Zevi writes in the *Enciclopedia Universale dell' Arte* (Institute for Cultural Collaboration, Venice, 1965): 'From the isolated blocks of the early villas, we pass to houses like Maser and Fonzolo, where the open appearance of the villa, extending through secondary buildings, is matched by the immersion of the architecture in the landscape.'

At Fratta Polesine (Rovigo), Andrea Palladio planned and built a villa (plate 18) for the Badoer family in the years 1568–1570. This was built in exact conformity to the original plans. Its outstanding features are the porticoed *barchesse,* which connect the building with its surroundings. The villa is a model of Palladian design in its simplicity and its use of characteristic architectural features. Also characteristic is the high pediment.

It is a very small building. The loggia has six columns, and leads back into a rectangular room intended to adjoin a rear porch (never in fact constructed) and a triple stairway. On either side are small rooms which communicate with the rectangular salon and contain the stairs. The granary is upstairs; the kitchen and cellars below.

In its vertical effect, too, the Badoera is a model Venetian villa; the proportions of the building are based throughout on human dimensions. The villa is built on deep foundations, and these provide the floor-level of the rooms.

The brothers Daniele Barbaro, patriarch of Aquileia, and Marc'Antonio Barbaro, diplomat and sculptor, were friends of both Palladio and Veronese. In the years 1560–1570 Palladio planned and built the Villa Barbaro at Maser for them (plates 20, 21 and 22) and Veronese did most of the interior decorations. It is the only Palladian villa of this period which has no porch, and the only one in which the private apartments of the *casa padronale* are sited on the upper floor of the *barchesse,* behind the arcades. The finest room in the villa is the garden-room, which leads from the cruciform hall into a little circular garden hollowed out of the side of the hill.

In the second book of his *Quattro Libri dell' Archi-*

tettura, Palladio gives this description of the ground-plan of the Villa Maser: 'The projecting part of the house has two rows of rooms. The upper floor is similar to the floor of the rear courtyard, which is cut out of the hillside. Near the house is a fountain with a wealth of painted and stucco decoration.

'This fountain makes a little lake, which is used for fishing. From this point the water flows into the kitchen-garden and then to the gardens on the right and left of the road, which rises gently to the house. It fills two fishponds above the highway, and then flows into the Bruolo, which is very large and full of good things.

'The façade has four Ionic columns. The capitals of the corner columns face in two directions, like those in the Book of Temples.

'On either side are loggias with dovecotes at the outside ends. Below these are rooms for wine-making, stables and other services.'

The villa is built on low, long lines in a vast park. The long rectangular main building, with octagonal rooms, corresponds to the central, cruciform front.

Most of the decorations inside the house are by Veronese, perhaps the first artist to paint figures on the *trompe-l'oeil* doors in order to achieve symmetrical effects.

The Villa Cornaro at Piombino Dese, Padua (plate 23) was built between 1560 and 1570, and is a fairly close realisation of the original plan. It has a square ground-plan with two very short wings. The façade at the rear of the building has a porch which leads to a square room with four columns, inspired by the Roman tetrastyle atrium. This room is the nucleus which governs the whole. The façade at the rear, which leads straight on to the natural surroundings of the building, is architecturally the most important feature. The Cornaro is very unusual among Venetian villas in having no lateral *barchesse*.

Another description by Palladio: 'Not very far from the Gambarare, above the Brenta, stands the house of the noble lords Nicolò and Luigi de Foscari (plates 25, 26 and 27).

'The house is raised eleven feet above the ground. Below, there are kitchens, servants' rooms and suchlike places, and the house is built so that lower and upper floors are identical.

'The main rooms have high ceilings, in accordance with the early method of calculating ceilings. The corner rooms have domed ceilings, and the ceiling of the salon is cruciform and semicircular. Its door-post is as high as the room, which is decorated with excellent paintings by Messer Battista Venetiano.

'Messer Battista Franco, the greatest artist of our time, had also begun to paint one of the great halls, but he died and his work remained unfinished.

'The colonnade is Ionic. The cornice continues all round the house, and forms a pediment above the loggia and on the opposite side. Under the eaves there is another cornice, which runs under the gables. The upper rooms seem to be cut in half and are . . . only eight feet high.'

Palladio's father apprenticed him as a stone-cutter to Bartolomeo Cavazza. He moved to Vicenza in 1524, where his new master was Giovanni da Porlezza, known as Pademuro. He worked there in obscurity until 1540; when he was working on the Villa Trissino the great humanist became interested in him, and thenceforth looked after him. In 1540, with the Villa Godi, now the Villa Valmarana, his professional career began in earnest. The Casa Civena at Vicenza and the Villa Marcello di Bertesina are also early works.

The Villa Godi (plate 24) consists of a group of buildings: the private apartments, the guest rooms, the riding-school and other subsidiary parts. The Valmarana family acquired the house in the 18th century, when Tiepolo did the frescoes. Characteristic features are the central part of the building, which is set back from, and higher than, the side wings. The original plan, however, presented a more clear-cut contrast between these two elements and the ground-floor. (This is the base of the house, which does not stand on plinths.)

Palladio's Rotonda belongs to the period when he was designing the Palazzo Chiericati at Vicenza. With these two buildings, he began the great period of his career, following them with the Villa Foscari, the Palazzo Valmarana and the Church of the Redentore at Venice.

Designed for Paolo Almerico, the Rotonda (plate 19) was sold after his death to the Capra brothers. It was begun in about 1550, and after Palladio's death Scamozzi was commissioned by Mario Capra to complete the building. It is incorrectly called 'La Rotonda' (a term used to describe buildings with a circular ground-plan) since the villa is clearly a parallelepiped. The design is, in fact, the intersection of a square with a cross.

Around a circular inner core like a great hall are distributed the other, identical, rooms on two perpendicular axes corresponding with the identical external façades. The main stairs, which might have broken the rigid symmetry of this plan, are in fact a feature of secondary importance, hidden away.

Around the villa is a panorama of trees, meadows and woods; and the extraordinary rapport between architecture and landscape is why this villa quickly became Palladio's best-known work, one which all cultivated European travellers have visited and praised.

Palladio worked alongside Vincenzo Scamozzi. Scamozzi designed two villas—the Villa Pisani at Lonigo and the Villa Duodo at Monselice—which are illustrated in this book. The Villa Pisani (plate 32) was planned in about 1576, and its appearance at once recalls Palladio's Rotonda, whose basic ground-plan Scamozzi borrowed. It has a circular domed room, at the centre of a square block, which acts as a pivot to the other rooms. These, however, are arranged differently from those in the Rotonda; the rear of the building ends in a porch, which is treated with much greater emphasis. The other façades were suggested by Serlio's designs.

Thus the plan of the Villa Pisani reveals profound differences from that of the Rotonda. There is an attempt to stress deliberately the complete block, eschewing Palladio's axial symmetry.

The Villa Duodo (plates 30 and 31) was built for Francesco Duodo in about 1592, on the site of an ancient chapel. It consists of two L-shaped blocks which enclose a rectangular courtyard. Facing this on the right is the chapel of S. Giorgio; on the left there is a broad flight of steps with the Rocca di Monselice behind.

THE CHATEAUX OF FRANCE

During the reign of Louis XI, there was a reawakening of artistic activity in France. As a result of Italian influence a taste for hunting-lodges and country homes became widespread. The valley of the Loire soon became the centre of this new development and some of the most splendid chateaux were built there. Intended for rest and recreation, they no longer had the grim look of fortified houses, and harmonised with their surroundings of parkland and streams. Gradually the rest of France followed the example of the Loire.

The early buildings (dating from the reign of François I) still have Gothic features, as in the châteaux of Blois, Chambord, Azay-le-Rideau and Chenonceaux; but the new architectural trend, strongly influenced by Italian practice, rapidly gathered strength.

The castle or château was the characteristic product of French secular architecture in the period under consideration. The following pages are devoted to the best-known and most characteristic examples of this type of building which, as in Italy, developed from a fortified house into a country retreat.

In the reign of François I French artists attempted to combine northern European features with those suggested by the new and powerful influences stemming from Italy. The spiral staircase of the chateau of Blois, for example, displays strong Medieval influence but also has monumental qualities typical of the art of the Italian Renaissance.

The ground-plan of the château of Chambord suggests that Leonardo may have had a hand in its lay-out, but Italian influence reached a peak in about 1570: France was invaded by Italian artists, who played a leading role in all the arts. Rosso Fiorentino (also known as Maitre Rous) and Primaticcio turned Fontainebleau into a centre for the practice and teaching of Italian art. Architecture was fundamentally changed by the work of Serlio, whose forceful personality was outshone only by that of the great Philibert Delorme.

Several French châteaux of the 15th and 16th centuries deserve slightly more detailed treatment. The château of Amboise (plate 34) is in Touraine.

Built in the Flamboyant style in about 1490, it was altered to include Renaissance features. The large airy rooms with rounded Italian Renaissance arches were unusual in contemporary French buildings, but rapidly became common thereafter. Amboise shows other signs of the general change of style. The wing facing the Loire, with its towers and galleries, and Louis XII's wing, with its fine round towers and a spiral staircase, are the architectural features most characteristic of the new Italian style.

The château of Chenonceaux (plate 35) was begun in 1513 and completed in 1521, though it retains a 15th-century keep; it is France's earliest Renaissance château. A long gallery on two floors, supported by five arches over the river Cher, was added to the main rectangular pavilion by Delorme.

Delorme is one of the greatest figures in 16th-century French humanism. Trained in his father's studio, he lived in Rome from 1533 to 1536. After brief visits to Florence and Lombardy, he returned to France and soon became very well known. The style he introduced was based on study of Classical art as well as the most important examples of Italian architecture; but it also took into account traditional building methods and specific local conditions and styles in the northern European countries. This is apparent in the arches of the château of Chenonceaux. The tradition stemming from Delorme's work was still strong enough to influence Jacques-Ange Gabriel in the second half of the 18th century.

Chambord (plate 36) is the most important of the châteaux in the valley of the Loire, which was the first part of France to absorb the Italian style. Begun in 1519 by François I, it has a simple rectangular ground-plan, with large round towers at the corners and a central residential block with a two-ramped spiral staircase.

The château of Blois (plate 37) was the favourite residence of the French kings throughout the Renaissance. It consists of a complex of buildings dating from different periods, grouped around an irregularly-shaped courtyard. Alongside Medieval features, Renaissance work is found in one wing, added by François I. Subsequently Mansart worked on the chateau. He was one of the first French architects to design ground-plan, constructional bearings and decorations, in his work on Gaston d'Orléans' wing (1636). This still follows the line of the old courtyard and the traditions of French 16th-century architecture. Its triumphal stairway anticipates the brilliance of the Escalier des Ambassadeurs at Ver-

17. Raphael (1483-1520). Villa Madama. Rome.

18. Andrea Palladio (1508-1580). Villa Badoer. Fratta
Polesine, Rovigo.

19. Andrea Palladio (1508-1580). Villa Capra, known as 'La Rotonda'. Vicenza.

20. Andrea Palladio (1508-1580). Façade of the Villa Barbaro. Maser, Treviso.

21. Andrea Palladio (1508-1580). Central façade of the Villa
Barbaro. Maser, Treviso.

22. Andrea Palladio (1508-1580). Wing of the Villa Barbaro.
Maser, Treviso.

23. Andrea Palladio (1508-1580). Villa Cornaro. Piombino
Dese, Padua.

24. Andrea Palladio (1508-1580). Villa Godi. Lugo Vicentino, Commune of Lonedo, Vicenza.

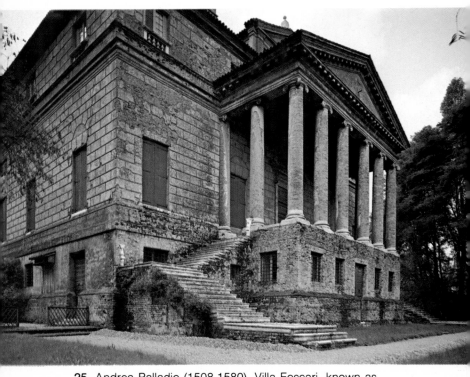

25. Andrea Palladio (1508-1580). Villa Foscari, known as
'La Malcontenta'. Mira, Commune of Malcontenta, Venice.

26. Andrea Palladio (1508-1580). Façade of the Villa Foscari, known as 'La Malcontenta'. Mira, Commune of Malcontenta, Venice.

27. Andrea Palladio (1508-1580). Rear of the Villa Foscari, known as 'La Malcontenta'. Mira, Commune of Malcontenta, Venice.

28. Baldassare Longhena (1598-1692). Villa Rezzonico, now
Villa Gasparini. Bassano, Vicenza.

29. Girolamo Frigimelica (1653-1732). Villa Toderini, now Villa Jelmoni-Bonicelli. Codogné, Treviso.

30-31. Vincenzo Scamozzi (1552-1616). Villa Duodo, now the Villa Valier. Side and front view. Monselice, Padua.

32. Vincenzo Scamozzi (1552-1616). Villa Pisani, known as 'La Rocca'. Lonigo, Vicenza.

33. Château de Fontainebleau.

34. Château d'Amboise. Touraine.

35. Château de Chenonceaux. Touraine.

36. Château de Chambord. Loire.

37. Château de Blois. Orléans.

38. Château d'Anet. Chartres district.

39. Wollaton Hall. Nottingham.

40. Burghley House. Stamford.

41. Kingston House. Bradford-on-Avon.

42. Hatfield House. Hertfordshire.

43. Longleat House. Wiltshire.

44. Villa Barbarigo. 17th century. Noventa Vicentina, Vicenza.

45. Giuseppe Piermarini (1734-1808). Villa Borromeo.
Cassano d'Adda, Milan.

sailles thirty years later, and other great achievements of French Classicism.

The building of the great château of Anet dates from 1547, when it was commissioned by Diane de Poitiers. Delorme was the architect. Although much altered in subsequent restorations, Anet reveals Delorme's greatness, demonstrating the skill with which he reconciled the architectural traditions of preceding centuries with Renaissance ideas.

The ground-plan is straightforward enough, but the details are executed with great stylistic freedom, and Delorme made use of volume and materials in a way that was unknown to the Middle Ages. The chapel was the first building with a round ground-plan to be constructed in France, and shows the influence of Bramante (S. Pietro in Montorio). The assurance with which Delorme introduced these new features, and his designs for the interior, testify to his greatness.

Fountainebleau, the residence of the kings of France, consists of a number of buildings from different periods—from 1100 to 1800—arranged on an irregular ground-plan. Gilles Lebreton, Serlio, Primaticcio and Jacques-Ange Gabriel were the most famous architects who worked there. The period of François I was the most important, Primaticcio being responsible for projects and buildings of considerable importance.

GREAT HOUSES OF ENGLAND

The new Italian style became popular in England too; but very few architects were ready to accept a complete break with tradition. There were three main sources on which English architecture drew in the 16th century: the early Italian Renaissance, the style of the Loire châteaux, and Flemish strapwork decoration. Among the most important achievements of the period are Burghley House, Longleat, Kingston House, Hatfield House and Wollaton Hall.

Burghley House (plate 40) was built by William Cecil, Lord Burghley, who was Queen Elizabeth's chief minister. The building is rectangular and measures 55 by 65 yards, with an inner courtyard. The most important feature of the courtyard is the tower, embodying French and Flemish characteristics.

One of the earliest buildings whose inspiration is really English is Longleat in Wiltshire (plate 43), begun in 1567 and built by Sir John Thynne with the help of the Queen's Master Mason, Robert Smythson. The façade is symmetrical, and uses all three orders on its pilasters, one order on each storey. The doorway, in the Italian style, is modestly proportioned and particularly dignified, with Tuscan Doric columns. There is not much decoration. The roof is flat and the windows rectangular, exemplifying the new trend—energetic, sober and unmistakably English —in English architecture. Longleat, like Wollaton Hall in Nottinghamshire, is a very big house; the arrangement of the grounds is unusual, and a great variety of effects is achieved.

The late 16th and early 17th centuries witnessed the rapid growth of the English country house. The impact of the Italian Renaissance was felt only slowly, but certain features of Italian architecture were gradually accepted and became integral parts of the English tradition. Ground-plans and elevations show a tendency to be symmetrical; the characteristics of the house, and particularly of the country house, undergo certain changes; and more importance is given to the rooms intended for private life, as opposed to those intended for public affairs. This altered relationship between the constituent parts of the country house is exemplified by the Great Hall of Hampton Court.

It was Inigo Jones and his pupil Webb who consciously introduced architectural features borrowed from Italy. Jones had begun his career as a designer of stage scenery, but became architect to Henry, Prince of Wales, and later to James I and Charles I. After two trips to Italy, he returned to England with a thorough knowledge of Palladian architecture. This taught him to think of a building as a whole, to understand the relationship between its different parts, to consider the arrangement of the ground-plan vis-a-vis the elevation, and to relate structure and decoration. 'Ye outward ornaments oft to be sollid, proportionalle according to the rulles, masculine, unaffected.' On this principle he based all his architecture. He introduced the formal Italian *discorso* (the love of symmetry, which he clearly derived from Palladio), revived traditional English values, and established a characteristic relationship between architecture and decoration, thus creating a new 'type' of English house. This had a rectangular ground-plan, evenly arranged windows, a straight cornice and a sloping roof; it was to influence the whole future development of English architecture.

THE BAROQUE, ROCOCO AND NEO-CLASSICAL PERIODS

Renaissance architecture was in the first instance an Italian phenomenon, but it was thereafter disseminated throughout Europe; France, England, Spain, Germany and Flanders were all strongly affected. It is therefore difficult to give a satisfactory description of the general artistic environment within which architecture developed between 1600 and 1900.

The customary division of these centuries into Baroque, Rococo and Neo-Classical periods is a convenient one, and corresponding changes in the character of country houses are worth pointing out.

It is necessary to distinguish between the larger stately buildings and humbler bourgeois dwellings, which had stronger connections with local or national tradition. The changes in the former were inconspicuous though not insignificant during the Baroque era, and very striking indeed after the advent of Neo-Classicism. The modification of typical features of the 16th-century house—Vignola's Villa Farnese at Caprarola, for example—is apparent in a Baroque house like Juvara's hunting-lodge at Stupinigi. But an Italian Neo-Classical building, still more an English or German example, has undergone major changes in structure and appearance.

The second group—the more modest residences—changed very little. The characteristics of such houses, from the farmhouse to the small bourgeois home, were largely determined by strong, essentially regional traditions which preserved their simple linear forms intact over the years.

At the end of the 16th century, Mannerism was replaced by a new artistic language: the Baroque. Bruno Zevi has pointed out the consequences: spatial freedom, freedom from conventions and rules, from symmetry, from the conflicting demands of internal and external space; restless energy, boldness, fantasy. Rome was at the centre of this artistic revolution, which was mainly promoted and fostered by the Church. It was a great age of religious architecture; the changes in secular architecture were decorative rather than structural, and were aimed at scenic effects of internal and external space. The Renaissance building centred on the courtyard was replaced by a building—town palace or suburban villa—centred on the *galleria,* a large room on the first floor. The building was no longer isolated in space: this was replaced by an attempt to create a naturalistic effect, the building itself becoming part of nature, or at least pervaded by the expressive freedom of nature. This style spread from Rome to

Northern Italy, and thence to Spain and Portugal, Germany, Austria, France and England.

The greatness of Bernini and Borromini in Italy was matched by that of Neumann in Austria and Pöppelmann at Dresden; the character of the villa was substantially changed by Pöppelmann's Zwinger, which will be discussed later.

After 1650, country houses were less important in France because the lives of the ruling classes were focused on the court. In England, by contrast, the aristocracy looked on their London houses as mere *pieds-à-terre,* and regarded their country seats as their real homes. At the end of the 17th century a standardised type of modest country house gradually came to be accepted throughout England. Built of brick, with stone pilasters at the corners, it was either completely rectangular or else had two short wings at the sides. The entrance was through a porch or portico, and there was another, larger portico at the centre of the façade. The earliest example is Eltham Lodge.

Of more grandiose buildings, Castle Howard and Blenheim Palace are closest to the great Baroque buildings of Italy (Stupinigi) and Germany (Zwinger) which have already been mentioned.

Neo-Classicism was born of a reaction against

Baroque and Rococo tendencies; it was a phenomenon of music and literature as well as the visual
arts. It was much more than an impulse to imitate
Classical art; it had its own creative force, which in
architecture led to the development of simple,
rational and functional forms. Appealing to the
simplicity of nature and the ascendancy of reason, the
Neo-Classical architects looked for rational qualities
in a building, for clear ground-plans, freshly related
proportions and a new simplicity of form.

Great masters of this phase were Valadier in
Italy, John Nash in England, and Gabriel in France.
Jacques-Ange Gabriel was the architect of the Petit
Trianon at Versailles (plate 53). It is a building without
projecting curves, cupola or even dormer windows;
it is small, cube-shaped, with only a few very restrained
decorations on its façade, and yet both vital and
charming. It is sometimes claimed that the Petit
Trianon shows the influence of English Palladianism,
but neither its general outline nor its detail appear to
offer any support for this view.

The generation after Gabriel—Soufflot, Ledoux
and Boullée—further developed the French Neo-
Classical country house. Ledoux, in particular,
undertook numerous commissions for town and
country houses; his design for a circular house for

the park-keepers at Maupertuis is particularly interesting.

Neo-Classicism was established in England by 1760. Robert Adam was its pioneer, and Lansdowne House and Syon House are among his most famous works. Outstanding in the next generation was John Nash, who designed the many houses around Regent's Park. Cronkhill, in Shropshire, built in 1802, has the shape of an Italian villa, with an arcade on slender columns and a sharply projecting roof. At Blaise Castle, near Bristol, on the other hand, Nash used the features of the old English country house, with its thatched roof and barge-boarded gables. For the Royal Pavilion, Brighton, he borrowed features from Indian architecture.

The new Neo-Classical spirit spread as far as Germany through the influence of English and Italian architecture. There is the Neo-Classical castle of Wörlitz, by the architect Erdmannsdorff, who designed a delightful house in the Italian style in the castle of Dessau. The predominant personality in this early period was Friedrich Gilly, an enthusiastic student of the Greek world, who designed a Gothic farmhouse in the park of the castle of Bellevue.

Karl Schinkel, who is considered the greatest German architect, was a pupil of Friedrich Gilly. In

Italy he studied Classical, Medieval and Renaissance buildings, and their relationship to the landscapes around them. The influence of Italian architecture is very clearly felt in the castle of Potsdam, as is that of Nash in the castles of Kurnik (now Kornik, Poland) and Babelsberg.

The work of Fischer von Erlach in Austria about the year 1690 signified the beginning of a great architectural tradition. In about 1700 he planned the Castle of Schönbrunn (plate 55) for the future Emperor Josef I. The building was to be completed by Pacassi, and was surrounded by a vast park intended like the castle to surpass Versailles. In its attempt to combine massiveness and solidity with a feeling for space and light, Schönbrunn had a strong influence on later castles in central and northern Europe.

The Zwinger at Dresden was built by Matthäus Daniel Pöppelmann for the Elector Augustus the Strong. Combining a conservatory with a stadium for tournaments and horse-riding, it consists of a single-storeyed loggia and two-storeyed pavilions. The line of the ground-floor arch is not regular; the first floor is open on all sides.

In his *Outline of European Architecture* (Penguin 1957) Pevsner writes: 'What an exultation in these rocking curves, and yet what a grace! It is joyful but never vulgar; vigorous, boisterous perhaps, but never crude. It is of an inexhaustible creative power, with ever new combinations and variations of Italian Baroque forms placed against each other and piled above each other. Borromini appears massive against this swiftness of movement through space.'

Villas belonging to the Baroque and Neo-Classical periods in Italy include the Villa Toderini at Codogné, the Villa Rezzonico at Bassano, the Villa Pisani at Stra and the Villa Barbarigo at Noventa Vicentina.

The Villa Rezzonico (plate 28), now the Villa Gasparini, was built in about 1600 and is attributed to a pupil of Scamozzi, Baldassare Longhena, who designed the dome of Santa Maria della Salute at Venice, as well as the Palazzo Rezzonico on the Grand Canal. The Villa Rezzonico is a rectangular building with four towers at its corners; its façades are severely designed, with very cautious use of decoration and few conspicuous features.

The ground-plan suggests that the design is derived from that of the oldest fortified houses, in which the towers leaned against the central block and were clearly defensive in function, facing the four points of the compass. This system was abandoned in Italian Renaissance villas, though it was widely used in French and English houses of the same period. The design of the interiors, however, has an altogether different emphasis, with clear stylistic affinities with the Baroque style, particularly in the design and lay-out of the park. The whole surrounding landscape is arranged with great tact to bring about a fusion of the building with its natural surroundings; this, as previously remarked, is a characteristic feature of the Venetian villa. The two side wings were built to a plan by Antonio Gaidòn; they play an important part in achieving the effect of the whole building dissolving into the landscape.

Girolamo Frigimelica was the architect of the Villa Toderini (plate 29) at Codogné, which was built around the year 1700. The main façade is very long, with a central block featuring a pediment rising above the rest of the building; two wings, which also end in pediments, recall the front of Palladio's Villa Barbaro at Maser.

But Frigimelica's villa is much heavier and more imposing. This is because of its dimensions rather than its design, which is light enough, with the central block not linked with the green parkland, but remaining somewhat cut off and detached from the side wings. The additional side buildings (the two *barchesse* and the chapel, which was restored in 1780) are very effective. They are clearly detached from the central building, and help to create an interesting panorama, aided by the different materials, the grass and the contrasting water of the lake. The design of the windows and the pilastered porticos soften the rigidity of the building, recalling the central block of the Villa Barbaro.

The Brenta Riviera is the final stretch of the river Brenta before it flows into the Lagoon. It was particularly celebrated in the 17th and 18th centuries as the 'playground of the Venetian aristocracy'. On the banks of the Brenta, at Stra, stands the Villa Pisani (plate 47), designed by Girolamo Frigimelica and Francesco Mattia Preti.

It lies at the centre of a large park, and is surrounded by subsidiary buildings which are complementary to the main block. It illustrates the lack of creative development in Italian architecture after the Baroque period. The massiveness of its construction is a good example of the ambitious spirit of the late Baroque.

This great mansion resembles Palladian villas in its ground-plan, while its elevation—on three floors, with half-columns supported by caryatids—belongs to the Baroque period. And the salon, with frescoes by Tiepolo, achieves a Baroque effect rather than a Rococo treatment of space. The main stable block, the porch and the maze are clearly the work of Frigimelica; the façade of the main building is by Preti, whose design was more severe and perhaps also more restrained than Frigimelica's original plan.

It is interesting to see how the interior proportions as well as the external appearance of this building result from the functions of the different parts. The lay-out of the great park retains many characteristic features of 17th-century Italian gardens, but is largely 18th-century in feeling.

As already remarked, the villa intended as a country house for rest and recreation did not develop in Lombardy during the Renaissance as it did in central and southern Italy. Nor was the 17th century one of great development, though the Palazzo Arese at Cesano Maderno, the Villa Belgioioso at Merate, and the Villa Crivelli at Inverigo deserve to be mentioned.

The architectural mood is very similar in all three houses. It was partly created by the transformation of an earlier building (almost always a castle), certain features of which are preserved in the ground-plan. Above all, in the careful treatment of the surroundings (gardens in the Italian style, etc.) these three houses share a characteristic which distinguishes them from comparable buildings in other parts of Italy.

It is only in the 18th and 19th centuries, with the establishment of the Neo-Classical style in Italy that there is a significant increase in the number of villas around Milan; these are situated along the main approaches (especially the rivers) and in the neighbourhood of Brianza. The Villa Visconti Majneri at Cassinetta, Villa Litta at Arcore, Villa Confalonieri at Verderio, Villa Vismara at Casatenuovo, 'La Gazzada' at Morazzone, and the Villa Taverna at Canonica al Lambro all belong to this fruitful period of Milanese architecture.

The Villa Borromeo at Cassano d'Adda (plate 45) was rebuilt in 1781 by Piermarini for the Marchese d'Adda. It was originally a castle, and was first altered by Croce for the Bonelli dukes; Piermarini's later renovation was fundamental, and completely altered the structure of the building.

It was planned and built after Piermarini had settled in Milan and become the city's most celebrated architect. He was a pupil of Vanvitelli, with whom he collaborated at Caserta, and introduced Neo-Classical principles to Milan and the rest of Lombardy. He also undertook to complete the town-planning work which Pellegrini had begun in Milan.

In the Villa Borromeo, we find some of the main features of Neo-Classicism: the cult of nature, of simplicity and purity of form; and a rational, functional attitude inspired by Greek and Roman examples. The building is U-shaped, in conformity to a ground-plan system which was very widely used in northern Italy. The central part is higher (three floors), and is connected with the sides by large arcades, a plan which also occurs in Venetian villas.

It was at this period that Milan regained prestige, and became a centre for Neo-Classical work. A process of renewal took place in architecture, sculpture and painting, beginning in the Neo-Classical period and being completed in Napoleon's time.

It was Piermarini who, in some thirty years of intense activity, changed the face of Milan, building La Scala, the Palazzo Grepi, etc., etc. His pupils, Pollak and Cantoni, followed his example. Milanese Neo-Classical architecture deserves attention, for it reflects the general trend of Neo-Classicism, albeit with certain local stylistic variations. It aimed at rationality, clarity in the arrangement of spaces, new proportions, simplicity of form, and symmetry. The overlapping of the Classical orders gave place to only one order of columns; the façade was often divided into three parts.

The Villa Belgioioso (plate 46) is the richest

46. Leopoldo Pollak (1751-1806). Villa Belgioioso. Milan.

47. Girolamo Frigimelica (1653-1732), Francesco Maria Preti (1701-1774). Villa Pisani. Stables and fish-pond. Stra, Venice.

48. Giuseppe Piermarini (1734-1808). Villa Reale. Monza, Milan.

49. Giuseppe Piermarini (1734-1808). Villa Reale. Monza, Milan.

50. Filippo Juvara (1685-1735). Hunting-lodge. Stupinigi, Turin.

51. Filippo Juvara (1685-1735). Hunting-lodge. Stupinigi, Turin.

52. The Orangery. Fulda.

53. Jacques-Ange Gabriel (1698-1782). Petit Trianon. Versailles.

54. Matthäus Daniel Pöppelmann. Zwinger. Dresden.

55. Fischer von Erlach. Castle of Schönbrunn. Vienna.

56. Villa Gallarati-Scotti. 17th century. Oreno, Vimercate, Brianza.

57. John Nash (1752-1835). Cumberland Terrace.
Regent's Park, London. Photo: John Webb.

58. Adam Brothers. Kenwood House. London.
Photo: John Webb.

example of the Neo-Classical villa. Its designer was Leopoldo Pollak, a pupil of Piermarini, with whom he collaborated on the rebuilding of the University of Pavia. The building faces one of the few curved streets in Milan—the Via Palestro—and has one completely open wall giving on to the public gardens.

When Pollak designed the building, however, the gardens had not yet been laid out. The house is U-shaped, following traditional Lombard villa design; the main front faced the existing garden and the other side faced the street. The main front is divided into two: there is a plinth below which is the ground-floor; above, the top two floors are joined by Ionic columns and pilasters. The garden, with the lake reflecting the outline of the building, with its undulations, winding paths, pleasantly sited woods and a stream, was also designed by Pollak.

The façade facing the street is set back and enclosed between two blocks, forming a courtyard. Towards the street this is bounded by a bossed wall; this has a central opening with three arches framed by Doric columns. The two wings of the U face the street, with three plain windows on the ground floor, and three with curved arches on the first floor.

On the ground floor, between the two wings facing the Via Palestro, two large vestibules—almost square, with an octagonal central space—open on to the courtyard. The three arches in the Via Palestro façade provide light for a rectangular ante-room with semicircular ends. On the garden side, there is a large salon with a vaulted ceiling. The staircase, restrained and elegant, leads to the first floor. The other rooms on both floors are less important and have been altered. The interior of the villa is decorated throughout, the most important works being the frescos by Appiani in the large salon on the first floor. They are among his finest works (*Apollo Playing the Lute, The Nine Muses*).

From 1777 to 1780 Piermarini planned and built the Villa Reale at Monza (plates 48 and 49). This is a work of the architect's maturity, and is impressive in its size and above all in its stateliness and the splendour of its surroundings.

The buildings containing the theatre and stables are at the side of the central block. Behind, hidden from view, are the subsidiary parts and the service quarters. The whole building, and especially the interior, displays late Baroque and Rococo influence. But the great salon, on two floors with a large balcony for the orchestra, and its great upper and lower vestibules, is typically Neo-Classical in feature and design. The park is later in date—and splendid: it is the nearest Italian equivalent to the gardens of Versailles and Schönbrunn.

Filippo Juvara, who lived in Turin from 1714 to 1735, planned and built the Palazzo Madama, the church of the Superga, and the hunting-lodge of Stupinigi. His masterpiece is Stupinigi (plates 50 and 51), which he planned and built in 1729 (long after the French and German equivalents, it must be remembered). Four wings in the shape of a St Andrew's cross are attached to the oval nucleus of the building. These enclose three courtyards: the first is semicircular and surrounded by buildings used as stables and kennels; the second is also semicircular; the third is the main octagonal *court d'honneur*.

The side facing the garden is the most impressive. Its sweeping lines reveal the vast expanse of the building, framed by the trees of the circular garden. When Juvara left Turin for Spain, the work was entrusted to Prunetto di Guarene, but both the lay-out of the central salon and the garden-plan are Juvara's. Stupinigi bears witness to the great ability of the Sicilian architect, and the influence of his work on the whole history of Italian Baroque.

In conclusion, it is necessary to touch upon the problem of the relationship between the architectural design and the formal distribution of interior space.

Consciousness of the problem in the West does not occur until the 16th century, when Serlio studied it. Even so, during the Renaissance there was a division of functions between the architect who designed the 'shell' and others who decorated and arranged the interior.

However, surroundings which aimed at intimacy, appropriately furnished, became more and more frequent. The Italian Mannerist country house was used as a place to stay, rest, work and entertain in; and concern for external design was linked with attention to convenience and comfort in the interior. In the Baroque period in Italy, little attention was paid to interior planning, and much that had been learned in the earlier period was overlooked or neglected. In France and England more concern was displayed, though interest in decoration predominated over distributive and functional planning. The Neo-Classical reaction was mainly stylistic; proportions and relationships were changed to give interiors greater dignity, but nothing was done to alter spatial distribution. In the 19th century the possibility of making use of various past styles which the architect could choose at will was exploited mainly by treating interiors and exteriors differently. It was at this time that the idea of 'furnishing styles', of the distinctions between a 'building', a 'room' and 'furniture' came into being. Architecture became a confused succession of styles borrowed from different times and peoples.

Around 1850, while building techniques were rapidly improving, the older artistic tradition moved into a state of crisis. The subsequent development of villa architecture, the resolution of the problem of interior space and the achievements of the Modern Movement will therefore be the subject of another volume in this series.

LIST OF ILLUSTRATIONS

1.　Villa Mirabello. 15th century. Milan. In this period country houses and hunting-lodges began to be built, as part of the changeover from the fortified to the residential house. The Villa Mirabello has an L-shaped ground-plan, its façade is entirely brick-covered, and it has high-arched terracotta windows.

2.　The courtyard of the Villa Mirabello. 15th century. Milan. Inside the Villa Mirabello three large arcades with stone columns open on to a courtyard. Architectural features derived from local tradition are noticeable; these had a strong influence on all Lombard domestic architecture, and were to recur in the early Renaissance châteaux of the Loire valley.

3.　Villa 'La Bicocca'. 15th century. Milan. The Bicocca of the Arcimboldi dates from the end of the 15th century. The windows are terracotta, with round and pointed arches. The building has been restored twice, first by Annoni and later by Portaluppi, and marks the beginning of Renaissance architecture. This can be seen in the belvedere on the top floor.

4. Bernardo Buontalenti (1536–1608). Villa di Artimino. Signa, Florence. Built for Ferdinand I, it stands on a hill in a vast pine forest. It is a very distinguished building, and is a splendid embodiment of late Renaissance style.

5. Bernardo Buontalenti (1536–1608). Villa di Artimino. Signa, Florence. The architect has attempted to combine the characteristics of the fortified house with those of the residential villa by means of dynamic elevations broken by numerous windows.

6. Bernardo Buontalenti (1536–1608). Villa 'La Petraia'. Florence. Built by Francesco dei Medici in 1575; the side facing the garden reveals that there was originally a castle on the site. When Buontalenti altered it, he retained the tower on the back wall, but made big changes in the general ground-plan. Typically 16th-century, the villa is centred on the court-yard, which leads to the reception rooms.

7.   Bernardo Buontalenti (1536–1608). Villa 'La Petraia'. Florence. All the natural features in the garden are arranged in a design which rigorously embodies the formal principles of the relationship between architecture and nature.

8.   Villa Gamberaia. Settignano, Florence. The site on which the villa was built belonged to the Gambarelli family of Settignano, which included the sculptors Bernardo and Antonio, who were known by the name of Rossellino. In 1592 the property was sold and the villa was transformed; the garden dates from the 17th century, and is laid out on different levels, with terraces alternating with woods in a highly complicated design.

9.   Villa Cicogna. 15th century. Bisuschio, Milan. Built as a hunting-lodge for the Mozzoni family; it is an outstanding example of the influence of Tuscan and Roman architecture on Lombard villas. The loggias of the wings recall Tuscan buildings. Other interesting features are the arcaded underground galleries and the staircase which leads into the garden.

10. Villa Cicogna. 15th century. Bisuschio, Milan. The building is arranged around a courtyard, in accordance with a ground-plan which is found in many Lombard villas; this type of building is clearly descended from the Medieval castle. In the garden, the varying levels of the hillside are used to good advantage, so that each floor of the house opens onto a different section.

11. Michelozzo Michelozzi (1396–1472). 'Il Trebbio'. Cafaggiolo, Florence. Built for Cosimo il Vecchio. This villa is an example of the attempt to combine Gothic features with those which more properly belong to the Renaissance. Originally designed as a hunting-lodge, it answered the humanist desire for a house which should be a place for the spirit to rest.

12. Giacomo Barozzi da Vignola (1507–1573). Villa Farnese. Caprarola, Viterbo. This is Vignola's masterpiece. It marks a decisive moment in the evolution of the Renaissance style towards Baroque, and is of great importance in the history of European architecture. The ground-plan is Sangallo's, but the transition from interior to exterior was created by Vignola by the insertion of a circular courtyard into the vast polygonal structure.

13. Giacomo Barozzi da Vignola (1507–1573). Villa Farnese. Caprarola, Viterbo. The semicircular courtyard at the centre of the building is surrounded by arcades which lead to the ground floor and first floor rooms. The elevation illustrates Vignola's stylistic severity, and its highly theatrical effect is characteristic of the architecture of the period. The floors are equally divided, and the imposing mass of the building is lightened by the graceful curve of the steps.

14. Giuliano da Sangallo (1445–1516). Villa Medici. Poggio a Caiano, Florence. This building was converted from the Strozzi family's Villa Ambra. The loggia which surrounds the whole *piano nobile* is the most striking change from the original structure; also important is the transformation of the central courtyard into a large salon two stories high. The garden was changed into a park in the English style during the 19th century.

15. Baldassare Peruzzi (1481–1526). 'La Farnesina'. Rome. This is the 16th-century version of the suburban villa, and consists of an angular central block which includes features dating from before the time of Bramante and Raphael; the central block is given extra visual interest by the receding middle part of the building and the two projecting side wings.

16.   Bartolomeo Ammanati (1511–1592), Giorgio Vasari (1511–1574), Giacomo Barozzi da Vignola (1507–1573). Villa Giulia. Rome. Vasari, Ammanati and Vignola collaborated on this design, and Michelangelo directed the work for Pope Julius II. Vasari was responsible for the general plan, Ammanati designed the central block, and Vignola the *nympheum*. The Zuccari brothers and Giovanni da Udine collaborated on the decoration of the interior.

17.   Raphael (1483–1520). Villa Madama. Rome. The Villa Madama is a poetic expression of the spirit of Renaissance man, with his admiration for Classical art. It announces the full flowering of the Renaissance villa, and influenced Palladio's designs. The semicircular façade is somewhat bare; the most impressive feature is the great loggia inside the villa. The decorations are by Giulio Romano and Giovanni da Udine.

18.   Andrea Palladio (1508–1580). Villa Badoer. Fratta Polesine, Rovigo. Built between 1568 and 1570, the Villa Badoer is a model of the Palladian Venetian villa. Its characteristics include simplicity in the use of architectural elements and lower proportions. Behind the six-pillared Ionic porch is an equally long rectangular salon, designed to lead to the rear porch, which was never built.

19.   Andrea Palladio (1508–1580). Villa Capra, known as 'La Rotonda'. Vicenza. The villa was begun in about 1550, and was finished by Scamozzi after Palladio's death. It has the two fundamental characteristics of the Venetian villa: a porch with Ionic columns on each of the four sides of the main building; and a carefully contrived harmony between the villa and its surroundings, which softens the somewhat theatrical effect of the whole.

20.   Andrea Palladio (1508–1580). Façade of the Villa Barbaro. Maser, Treviso. Built between 1560 and 1570, the inside of the house was decorated by Veronese, like Palladio a friend of the two Barbaro brothers; the frescoes he painted in the Villa were extremely influential on later Venetian art.

21.   Andrea Palladio (1508–1580). Central façade of the Villa Barbaro. Maser, Treviso. Conceived and planned on low lines, and extended into the vast park, the façade of the Villa Barbaro stands free of the main block of the building. The complex ground-plan consists of a rectangular building, with perpendicular rooms on the longitudinal axis, and a projecting central block which serves as a reception room.

22.   Andrea Palladio (1508–1580). Wing of the Villa Barbaro. Maser, Treviso. The circular chapel of the villa is also the work of Palladio, and was apparently inspired by the Pantheon at Rome. The proportions of the porch, the projecting chapels, and the lowered interior arches are original Palladian features which differ markedly from the Pantheon.

23.   Andrea Palladio (1508–1580). Villa Cornaro. Piombino Dese, Padua. The villa has a rectangular ground-plan, with two very short wings and a site which is open in front of the building. The square salon is the heart of the building, and communicates with the other parts; the rear façade is in close touch with the surrounding landscape, and is architecturally the most important feature. There are no farm buildings, usually essential features of a Venetian villa.

24.   Andrea Palladio (1508–1580). Villa Godi. Lugo Vicentino, Commune of Lonedo, Vicenza. The Villa Godi is one of a group of buildings dating from about 1540; it is believed to be Palladio's earliest work. The building no longer follows the original design: the central block and the two projecting wings comprise a ground-plan differing from Palladio's.

25. Andrea Palladio (1508–1580). Villa Foscari, known as 'La Malcontenta'. Mira, Commune of Malcontenta, Venice. Planned and built around 1555, while Palladio was still working on La Rotonda and the Villa Maser.

26. Andrea Palladio (1508–1580). Façade of the Villa Foscari, known as 'La Malcontenta'. Mira, Commune of Malcontenta, Venice. This famous example of the temple-villa, planned around a central cruciform space, faces the waters of the Brenta, The natural setting is indeed a splendid one, flooded with light.

27. Andrea Palladio (1508–1580). Rear of the Villa Foscari, known as 'La Malcontenta'. Mira, Commune of Malcontenta, Venice. In the rear façade, too, we observe the motif—also present at the front—of the pediment, which emphasises the vertical thrust of the walls. This, as well as the rigorous axial symmetry, is characteristic of Palladian design. The interior is decorated with frescoes by Giovanni Battista Zelotti and Battista Franco.

28. Baldassare Longhena (1598–1692). Villa Rezzonico, now Villa Gasparini. Bassano, Vicenza. The exterior is plain, and its imposing austerity recalls the original castle. The interior (central salon and *scalone d'onore*), however, demonstrates that brilliant effects were aimed at. A very interesting feature of the whole building is the way in which it is integrated with its surroundings.

29. Girolamo Frigimelica (1653–1732). Villa Toderini, now Villa Jelmoni-Bonicelli. Codogné. Treviso. The villa, attributed to Frigimelica, was built for the Toderini counts. The design recalls the Villa Barbaro at Maser in the predominance of the façade and its division into three main parts, the central part taller than the others. The remarkable elevation is toned down by the clear delineation of the three sections with their matching pediments.

30. Vincenzo Scamozzi (1552–1616). Villa Duodo, now the Villa Valier. Side view. Monselice, Padua. Arranged in two L-shaped blocks facing a rectangular courtyard, the house has been attributed with assurance to Scamozzi, though some parts are by Andrea Tirali. Near the building are six small chapels and a little church, also the work of Scamozzi.

31.   Vincenzo Scamozzi (1552–1616). Villa Duodo, now the Villa Valier. Front view. Monselice. Padua. The whole architectural complex, in the setting of the Rock of Monselice, is matched in beauty by the surrounding landscape. The style shows some Palladian influence.

32.   Vincenzo Scamozzi (1552–1616). Villa Pisani, known as 'La Rocca'. Lonigo, Vicenza. 'La Rocca' has a domed circular salon situated in the centre of a square. There is a porch only on the south side, where it is inserted in the line of the façade. The architectural image anticipates 18th-century Neo-Classicism.

33.   Château de Fontainebleau. Fontainebleau consists of a very irregular arrangement of buildings from different periods, from 1100 to 1870. Its most brilliant age was when François I chose it as his favourite palace. France's most famous architects worked there: Gilles le Breton in 1528 (ballroom), Primaticcio (the 1568 wing), Delorme (Henri II's ballroom) and Gabriel (the monumental stairway, 1642).

34. Château d'Amboise. Touraine. Amboise became the favourite country residence of the kings of France, and Renaissance art flourished there. The château, now partly destroyed, is Flamboyant in style; Renaissance elements added in about 1490 include the wing which faces the Loire and that of Louis XII, with round towers and a spiral staircase.

35. Château de Chenonceaux. Touraine. Chenonceaux is one of the earliest French Renaissance châteaux. It consists of a rectangular pavilion to which Delorme added a long gallery and two storeys on arches over the river Cher. It is interesting to see traditional Gothic construction and decoration side by side with features added by Delorme after his Italian travels.

36. Château de Chambord. Loire. Chambord is the most important of the Loire châteaux. It has a regular rectangular ground-plan, with large round towers at the corners of the building and a massive central dwelling block divided vertically by a broad, two-ramped spiral staircase. The pinnacled roof, with its chimneys and dormer windows, shows the influence of the Medieval French and Lombard traditions.

37. Château de Blois. Orléans. The château of Blois is Merovingian in origin and stands at the confluence of the Loire and the Arrou. It consists of buildings arranged around an irregular courtyard. Some of the surrounding towers are 13th-century; the entrance wing was built in 1440. In 1579 the adjacent wing, inspired by Renaissance Lombardy, was begun. Louis XIII later carried out general reconstruction work to Mansart's designs.

38. Château d'Anet. Chartres district. Philibert Delorme began this great château for Diane de Poitiers in 1547. It was destroyed during the 19th century. The cryptoportico remains, as do a restored side wing and the domed chapel.

39. Wollaton Hall. Notts. This building is still in the Gothic style, which never entirely disappeared in England. The house includes features from the three mainsprings of English architecture of this period: the early Italian Renaissance, the style of the Loire châteaux, and Flemish strapwork. These were accompanied by a traditional interest in picturesque and asymmetrical effects.

40.   Burghley House, Northants. A vast rectangular building, measuring some 160 feet by 200 feet, with an interior courtyard. The central feature of this courtyard is a three-storeyed pavilion, built in 1585, which follows the lines of the French triumphal arch, with pairs of niches and columns. The three orders are correctly used, but there is an incongruous projecting window between the columns on the third floor.

41.   Kingston House. Bradford-on-Avon, Wilts. This house is in the late Perpendicular style. Later features, painfully applied in a 'Gothic' manner, are the façade, the windows, the finials and the projecting bays.

42.   Hatfield House. Herts. The doorway is very small in proportion to the rest of the building. The flat roof, the geometrical effect created by the front, and the large area taken up by the windows makes a curiously modern impression. This house also includes features from French and Italian architecture which are not, however, successfully blended.

43. Longleat House, Wilts. Begun in 1567, Longleat is typically Elizabethan; only the modestly-proportioned doorway is Italian in style. Decoration is very sparingly used. Severely rectangular, with a flat roof and many oblong windows against flat surfaces, Longleat creates an almost 20th-century effect.

44. Villa Barbarigo. 17th century. Noventa Vicentina, Vicenza. Built by Barbarigo at the beginning of the 17th century. The broad façade, with its surprising vertical development—a new feature in Venetian architecture—has a projecting, two-storeyed central porch and two receding wings. The loggias of the wings provide the main architectural interest.

45. Giuseppe Piermarini (1734–1808). Villa Borromeo. Cassano d'Adda, Milan. This was originally a castle, and was first altered by Croce. Piermarini radically changed the whole structure, elegantly linking the three-storeyed central block with two L-shaped side wings by means of three arcades.

46. Leopoldo Pollak (1751–1806). Villa Belgioioso. Milan. U-shaped, in accordance with Lombard villa tradition, the house has its main front on the garden, and the other on the street. The main façade is divided horizontally into two; the ground floor below, and a single unit above, two storeys high, with Ionic columns and pilasters. The complex façade facing the street is set back, and is enclosed between two blocks which form a courtyard leading to the large ground floor halls.

47. Girolamo Frigimelica (1653–1732), Francesco Maria Preti (1701–1774). Villa Pisani. Stables and fish-pond. Stra, Venice. The Villa Pisani, in the centre of a large park and surrounded by subsidiary buildings, faces the banks of the Brenta. The ground-plan belongs to the Palladian tradition, while the exterior is typically Baroque.

48. Giuseppe Piermarini (1734–1808). Villa Reale. Monza, Milan. One of Piermarini's mature works, the Villa Reale is impressive in its size and above all in the dramatic arrangement of its surroundings. The great central block is bounded by complementary wings which house the stables and theatre. At the rear are subsidiary parts and service quarters.

49. Giuseppe Piermarini (1734–1808). Villa Reale. Monza, Milan. The view that Piermarini was careful about form and composition, but not over-gifted with imagination, is confirmed by this façade, loaded with borrowings from Vanvitelli. The park, which is later in date, is a wonderful piece of landscape-gardening, and can compare with Le Notre's Versailes and Von Erlach's Schönbrunn.

50. Filippo Juvara (1685–1735). Hunting-lodge, Stupinigi, Turin. Juvara's masterpiece: it has the stamp of modernity, far from the visual tradition of French architecture. The central nucleus is an oval, from which four wings branch out diagonally.

51. Filippo Juvara (1685–1735). Hunting-lodge. Stupinigi, Turin. The building includes three courtyards: the first is semi-circular and is surrounded by stables and kennels; the second is also semicircular; the third is octagonal. Charles André Van Loo, Angelo Del Vacca and Giovanni Battista Crovato collaborated on the interior decorations.

52.   The Orangery. Fulda. Belongs to the eclectic period of German architecture. This detail of the great German palace shows elements still influenced by Medieval Gothic, while the ground-plan is typically 17th-century, and the Rococo style is superimposed on the façades.

53.   Jacques-Ange Gabriel (1698–1782). Petit Trianon. Versailles. This is a building without obtrusive curves or cupolas. It is a small cube, gay and charming; there is a minimum of restrained decoration on the façade. It is not influenced by English Palladianism.

54.   Matthäus Daniel Pöppelmann. Zwinger. Dresden. The Zwinger is a combination of a conservatory and a stadium for tournaments and horse-riding. It consists of a single-storeyed gallery and two-storeyed pavilions. The first floor is open on all sides.

55. Fischer von Erlach. Castle of Schönbrunn. Vienna. The castle was built for the future Emperor Josef I, and was to express in architectural terms the supremacy of Imperial authority.

56. Villa Gallarati-Scotti. 17th century. Oreno, Vimercate, Brianza. The original plan of the villa dates from the second half of the 17th century. It was afterwards changed, but the park remains; here, in a theatrical and Arcadian atmosphere, is the *nympheum* of Neptune, a complex and heavy construction which is typical of the Baroque period.

57. John Nash (1752–1835). Cumberland Terrace. Regent's Park, London. Photograph: John Webb. Designed by the most famous English architect of his time. It includes striking 18th-century features and, as a monumental piece of town-planning, looks forward to the idea of the garden-suburb.

58. Adam Brothers. Kenwood House. London. Photograph: John Webb. This is typically English architecture, with its alternating rising and falling lines of projecting and receding parts. It is a long way from the spirit of Classicism and from the aesthetics of the Palladian and Baroque styles.